CLARENCE THOMAS

The Things He Learned

L. D. Hicks

A POST HILL PRESS BOOK
ISBN: 978-1-64293-619-3

Clarence Thomas:
The Things He Learned
© 2021 by L. D. Hicks
All Rights Reserved

Cover and Interior Illustrations by Darwin Marfil
Cover Design by Cody Corcoran

Post Hill Press
New York • Nashville
posthillpress.com

Published in the United States of America

1 2 3 4 5 6 7 8 9 10

Printed in Canada

To my beautiful Lisa.

852

When Clarence Thomas was a little boy, he went to live with his grandparents, Anderson and Tina.

Anderson taught Clarence and his brother that working hard was good.

Life was not easy for African-American
children when Clarence was growing up.
In fact, they made laws that kept the
races separate!

These laws were terribly mean,
weren't they?

African Americans could not use
the same bathrooms, go to the same
schools, or even eat in the same places
as white Americans.

Clarence Thomas' grandfather wanted
Clarence and his brother to be successful
no matter what.

He taught them that to be successful they
had to work harder than anybody else, no
matter what color their skin was. He made
sure Clarence and his brother always went
to school!

Anderson Taught Clarence and his
brother how to build a house...

...drive an oil truck, work on
a farm, and give to those who
needed help.

Clarence went to private Catholic school and his teachers were nuns and priests. While he was in school, he learned math, manners, memorization, and that it was okay to be different and think for yourself!

Clarence had perfect attendance at school
and was never late to class. The nuns, like
Clarence's grandpa, believed that failure was
not an option!

Clarence loved to read. In fact, his friends were sometimes disappointed that he would rather read or study than play outside!

Even though Clarence loved to study,
he also loved to play basketball!

He could dribble!
He could spin!
He could do tricks!

He had fun showing off!

In 1964, Clarence Thomas went to high school and learned about Martin Luther King Jr. and what it's like to be mistreated because of the color of your skin (that's called racism).

He also learned the difference between right and wrong, and that all kids could go to school together.

Clarence's high school was an all-boys boarding school where black students and white students lived and studied together.

Sometimes, the white kids made ugly jokes and were mean. Clarence Thomas learned about bullies and how to stick up for himself by working hard no matter what!

Sports were important to Clarence.
Not only was he smart, he was a
good athlete!

After graduating from high school, Clarence Thomas went to college. Clarence learned how to stand up for his beliefs and teach others to understand his point of view.

When he was in college, Clarence Thomas studied very hard, just like when he was younger. He learned a lot about words and writing. He also learned how to run a newspaper.

After many years in school, Clarence Thomas learned enough to be a lawyer! He used everything he learned to help people, just like his grandfather taught him.

In 1974, Clarence Thomas worked for the state of Missouri. He worked hard and learned about the Republican Party, which is a group of people in government who shared his way of thinking.

He learned that he could still impress his friends at basketball and that all people don't have to think the same.

He knew his grandfather was right to teach him the value of hard work.

After a while, Clarence Thomas went to work for an office of the government that makes sure that all people are given a chance to find good jobs, no matter what color their skin might be. This was called the Equal Employment Opportunity Commission and Clarence was in charge.

While he was there, he learned that all people should be treated the same in the workplace.

He believed that people should be able to take care of themselves and each other, and that the government should help when life was hard.

In the United States there is one job that is guaranteed for life: a Supreme Court Justice! Only nine people in the United States have this job at one time, and the President of the United States has to nominate you for it!

On July 1, 1991, President George
H. W. Bush nominated Clarence
Thomas for the Supreme Court!

Out of thousands of people the
President chose Clarence Thomas!

The Supreme Court is in charge of all the courts in the United States, and nine judges are in charge of the court. The judges sit at the head of the courtroom on benches and wear black robes. The judges are like basketball referees and make sure that everyone plays by the rules.

US Supreme Court

Lawyers argue people's disagreements in front of the judges and a group of people called a jury decide which side wins.

The Supreme Court makes decisions for the whole country!

On October 23rd, 1991, Clarence Thomas was sworn in as the 106th Justice of the Supreme Court. A once-in-a-lifetime opportunity!

As a Supreme Court Justice,
Clarence Thomas learned
to understand laws passed
by Congress, to listen to
lawyers debate both sides
of the law, and to decide
which side wins!

The Supreme Court was created 232 years ago! Since then, only 115 people have been chosen to be Justices on the Supreme Court. That is how special a job Clarence Thomas has!

115 Justices

232 Years

Clarence Thomas is still a Supreme Court Justice today.

He used everything he learned in life to be successful.

Learning is important.

What have you learned today?